Blue Muse Rising

John Schulte

BLUE MUSE RISING

First Pangea Press edition.

An imprint of Pangea Publishing
Dana Point, California 92629

ISBN-10: 0-9894065-6-3

ISBN-13: 978-0-9894065-6-7

This book is set in Garamond.

Dedication

This book is especially dedicated to you.
You know who you are.

And...

To Blythe —
music diplomat and daughter,
who heals wounded hearts with her divine voice.

To Cheryl —
creator, wife, and mother,
who connects the stars with her grace.

To Lee —
thanks for being my Ezra!

To the Family —
continually, the backbone of it all,
whose support and inspiration are without limits.

To Little Dog —
for the necessary and incessant mocking.

Apologies

To everyone who hates poetry,
which is not as many people as you think.

Universal and elusive, everywhere and nowhere —
these are the musical bars of poetry that sing their
truth the moment they're born, whenever that may be.

Preface

Poetry is always new. It is never read as it was intended. It freshens itself by its mere existence, time after time. But you may still enjoy poetry in profound ways that were never intended and that may transcend the inspiration of its inception. For those images and metaphors, which excite sensations that you've never known, are stabs of joy, impaled into the soul by a bleeding blade that heals the wound as it exits. A flash of light and thunder that is seen only for that one instance: Crystalline, pure, and original for only that moment and never again fresh in the same way, never again the same euphoria.

The recurrent longing for sublime joy resurrects the inherent nostalgia for life's meaning. Poetry, like music, possesses the power to conjure up a fleeting glimpse of that elation through the window of glory, each time a new awakening shines through. A new truth or a new fiction. Perhaps an epiphany that lingers and becomes a lasting inspiration.

We ache to be on the other side of the glass, which becomes a curtain of gloom that cloaks our view nearly the moment we experience the treasured image.

This is the essence of ecstatic melancholy, sublime happiness that connects us to creation itself, even if for only a brief moment. This is the alchemy of clarity and meaning struggling to remain alive, but swiftly dissolving into a shroud of chaos.

Some poems have that power. It depends on you; it depends on the poem. It depends on the moment. Perhaps something in this collection will pierce your spirit; if not, look elsewhere for language that stimulates and brings you to the brink of uncharted and rapturous consequences. For, indeed, the ephemeral, ungratified desire is always far more satisfying than any tangible pleasure. It's not what you read; it's what you perceive in what you've read. That's poetry.

BLUE MUSE RISING

Poetic Dust That Connects Us

John Schulte

10-10

Rhythm overwhelms the miracle you are
The beating heart that fired into being
was once only a loose grip of prayer
that tenderly took hold and would not let go
like interlaced hands in the abbey of your soul

Your pulse consumes the miracle you are:
Persistent and hallowed, profoundly consistent
a blessing of form so perfectly designed
a treasure of boundless glory whose rapturous
first breath was a symphony of life

Your presence assumes the miracle you are
Like a precious petal on the bloom of Creation
it is a joy to behold the unfolding wonder
and the awakening to your own power of light
Your gift is to accept the miracle you are

42

Each time the enigma is solved

the answers all swiftly dissolve.

Philosophers may grow weary

by this unusual theory —

explain the inexplicable

and watch it turn more quizzical!

Oh, we have known so many times

why we're here and what's over there.

But logic dictates dreams are crimes —

best to wonder and always stare:

What you imagine may be true

but beware the ol' switcheroo!

Apollo's Swan Song

The stars are falling like rain

dropping a brilliant blaze into darkness,

leaving a blanket of mottled nothingness

in their faded rippling wake.

Once faithful and inspiring,

they descend into a dance

without destiny, dying embers

that were once afire with dreams.

Each extinguished star

is a calm heart thrumming to its end,

a spirit coming to a final rest,

after shining a comforting glow.

Astrolabing

When the marbles splattered through space,

when souls became frenzied faces,

when eyes viewed the atomic dance,

when design bowed to random chance,

when your body nervously rose,

when your warm heart quivered and chose —

those were the moments that mattered,

as molecules bumped and scattered.

The mind-forged fragrance of order,

the shapes sans base, bind, or border,

The crude chaos of miasma —

freedom orbits around plasma...

Every womb is a universe;

divided cells richly diverse;

sheer darkness comforts and protects;

mere fearless innocence reflects;

unborn, light and marvels of life;

unknown majesty, unknown strife;

readied by mystery, forced to leave;

behold the blaze, embrace, believe;

prepare for life and then your death:

fear releases first and last breath.

Autumn is Brewing

Mahogany and maple trees
dressed like shivering clowns
rustle and crackle as scurrying
nutbrown squirrels nestle-in
a knot for a chilly night.
A trail of fire streams down the waterfall
disappearing into a crust of frost below.
The smoldering ash of the fireplace
glowers deeply up the chimney
angered that its embers are fading.
Inside, children grab golden pears
and crispy apples from the cornucopia
all the cascading colors of the Fall
spilling out as the layered coats of leaves
outside cast off and swirl down the trunks,
becoming variegated tree aprons.
The squirrels find their buried seeds
as the children color with crayons
before taking their last nap
in the old woman's cabin.

Becoming Well-Versed

I will not be constrained
by sonnets or quatrains;
I shall not follow rhyme,
adhere to meter time;
my verse must be kept free
to show the best of me.
No pen for acrostic —
a form that's so caustic;
no storied love ballad,
nor anything hallowed;
breaking apart concrete,
not one line's a repeat....
And poems that are epic
are fittingly septic.
For ev'ry elegy
comes an apology.
Who wants to break the code,
dissect an awful ode?
No running the gauntlet
in search of a couplet.
Of all the rhetoric
Please, please no limericks.
And I shan't write haiku —
5-7-5 adieu!

A Bird with Wings

He is clearly hard at work,

surrounded by an hourglass;

he's going to the Gala

with blood on his hands;

Mediterranean milk and symbolic fish

splatter from the birthing egg;

he doesn't care what you say

— yet he asks for your advice,

though he truly only needs an accomplice.

His profound secret influence

shall remain profoundly secret

and very influential.

He will never be a cook,

nor ever go to Waterloo....

But he is inspired by everything....

And when he reaches out for perfection

he touches the hand of Raquel Welch.

Blocked

The blank page waits patiently, like Zen,

while the prison of perception peers out the ol' State Pen:

No ink can dink a do.

What's a po' boy without a shoe

to polish unless he's Polish?

You can only sell a cell to the foolish.

The walls are scratched with scribbles

and etched with scrawled fribbles,

doddered doodles of days gone by,

from inmates who were Frenched then fried.

Then it comes to me, so swift, so clear:

I gotta get out of here!

The words are not within the confines of my mind

they float through the steel bars and waft to the stars.

I pray to a charcoal sketched Shroud of Turin

whilst standing in my cellmate's puddles of urine.

I gotta get out of here and unwind,

but leaving means going out of my mind.

Bonds of Union

I could write The Idiot

    or orchestrate Pictures at an Exhibition;

I could paint the Mona Lisa

    or draw Bugs Bunny;

I could compose Carmina Burana

    or indite the Four Quartets;

I could cogitate on a theory of relativity

    or strangle women in Boston;

I could torture and incinerate Jews

    or set fire to Rome;

I could and I can

    because I am a human being.

Channeling Christopher Smart

This is where I am.

Where is Jerusalem when it matters?

The Lord was born unto Boston

to set the sail crisp and proper

Let no ale put asunder the wave of Glory

for the past has undone the present

with its mockery of Fate

Oh Fortuna how doth thou breathe

when the lungs of fire are in-folded

and the depths of Hell are extended

for those who choose to arrest their convictions?

Seek now a final resting place

for the home cannot find its foundation

The left is far from right

and what is over is under the bridge

and the fountain of all bereavement

is but a trickle upon the withered Earth

Let us all soak into the stain of existence

as Judas has allowed his honor to be soiled

before Man and God and angel alike

Let not all the choirs sing forth

for they shall only praise the horrors of

your own divine sanctity, which is noble to ye

but unworthy of a place in the Kingdom

For thine is the Kingdom

Tender is the dove that takes flight with your dreams

Holy is your rumination that makes life a flattering affair

that trims the wide turns of the gyre into tight circles of delight

Blessed be you the sacred Lamb of Jerusalem

Blessed be you, Oh babe of Bostonian heritage

Blessed be your mark upon this Land

Blessed be the land we walk upon

Blessed be the aching of heart

Blessed be the heart that feels nothing

Blessed be the heart the feels it all

Blessed be your solemn quest

Blessed be the final days before the Fall

When the crown of thorns are thrust

Upon the fierce cold of a once warm body

It is sad

It is dead

It is over

Tears are the flood and Boston is the city

I have never known Boston as I have known

The City I have never visited: Jerusalem come!

The fleece on his back is slick and righteous

The nape of his neck is soft and aglow

The firmament is tainted with his presence

For it knows that the starkness of dark

Shall not bury the furtive heart

It is lost in turmoil! It is gone!

Gone! But lost!

So it can no longer last to be found

by the souls of those confined in the chambers

Let them cry to be free

Let them try

For you must break the artifice

Tear down the roses from their trellis

as they point in the directions of your salvation

You shall overcome

You shall be there

You shall inherit the cause

You shall burst into a million stars

You shall light the vast blanket of darkness!

Oh hail! Oh joy! Oh Master seek it all!

Do you not love me?

Of course you do

Then I love you

For it is a simple exchange

So ripe! So moist! So ready for the plucking
Take! Eat! Now go and tell all of my Glory
You bastards — one and all.

Connections

Anne's willing womb bears fruit

that ripens and rots to the root

in the stunning orchard

of the innocently tortured.

Prolapse twins set your stage,

casts your fate with umbrage:

Your heart has room

to accept the doom —

and embrace new faces

whose parental traces

are mired in mystery

and puzzling history.

Guilty and guiltless fry side-by-side;

a forced homicide

from the gentlemen of Venona:

"We're gonna kill ya!"

Sing! Sing! Have mercy on us all!

They cannot walk before they crawl.

Let them teach you a thing or Jew...

as they are taken from public view.

Maybe the mister, unlike his sister, was a spy

if you can believe the lie:
The tinted Greenglass
obscures the betrayal of his past —
a legal lynching
with no strange fruit from the trees,
no swinging from the changing breeze.
Percolating brains leave steaming stains
and the not-so-sudden smell of burning flesh —
the gift of a deceptive brother who later confessed.

Delivering sovereignty from the glare of rockets —
still, no birds can pluck from empty sockets,
nor see the visions and dreams
once pitifully plugged with eye screams.
The shadow of the bomb,
a mushroom of calm,
explodes with paranoia
as ravenously intense as Goya.
The tearing fears on an international front
rip to reveal the magic of a witch hunt.
You are part of this now, your life co-opted:
Their future is yours, adopted.
You are not Saturn, your fatherly instincts
intact, no longer extinct.

For without the execution,

without the restitution,

you are empty, withered, and embittered.

But you pick the etrog, the citron

as if it has grown from the Jaffa shoreline;

and you raise the fruit from the leafy boughs,

as the willows of the brook caress and endows,

delivers us from evil, from our hellish flaw —

for in their ripening, is absolution, hope for us all!

A Currency of Likes

No one cares what you peck.
No one reads what you write.
Yet you stick your thick neck
on the block's bloody site.

People scroll past your thought.
People mistake what's said.
What ideas hath you wrought?
The art of discourse, dead.

A thousand responses,
Deafness from the noises.
Pros, cons, and renounces
when everyone voices.

It's chimpanzee simple:
Make it all right, click Like.
Costs less than a thimble —
thumbs up world, take a hike.

D.C.

The gift was chillingly apropos:

William Wilson, don't you know.

His vain attempts to flee his natal roots

for the deadly embrace of a blonde Medusa,

whose looks elicited hoots,

but whose alluring lips of fuchsia

now rot faster than her celluloid.

His ex, a tawdry Jezebel who destroyed

his hope of being a happy father and husband,

ironically in her denial of his love, he has been

raised up with new powers of expression to levels

that surpass his dreams and exorcise his devils.

But like William Wilson whose life was ended

by William Wilson, this man so nobly descended.

Death, O Where Doth Thou Stop?

She died on the train to Aberdeen.
We left her at Waverly Station.
Words were never exchanged.

She drank her coffee,
then fell asleep.
Stonehaven is a stop
on the way to Aberdeen.

The steward tallied her up
among the living —
but will the train police
demand a ticket?
Is she entitled to a refund?

The sky is very blue here,
the grass so very green;
and death does not stop
on the way to Aberdeen.

DeMused

You're back again
because you never left.
Haunting my heart
and corrupting my soul....
I try not to listen
to your undermining tone;
but it's coursing through my veins
like a winding road unwinds
under cloudless midnight rains.
Flooding memories wash away
the pain you always bring;
then the morning dew glistens
as I welcome you home
like streaking rays of hope....
So I'm never left alone
with your self-defeating jeer;
and just as I complete a thought
you say, "I'm here, I'm here!"
And where to place the blame?
What's done comes undone —
Unravels like a ball of shame:
I feel my pulse and I'm the one.

Disturbing the Peace

So little depends

upon

a red envelope

hongbao

brimming with change

coins

next to the olive

tank

Gong Xi Fa Cai!

The freedom dragon enters

while eager hands hold their treasure;

then over the air,

under the cerulean sky,

the quiet revolution —

Transformers transform.

The gifts afford a new treasure:

Triggerbots for little tots

More Than Meets The Eye!

To get rich is glorious

but some feel the glory before others

After the peddling comes the pedaling
for faster, faster, faster Wéixīn!
Flying Tigers bicycle in circles around the Square.
Oh, Goddess of Democracy!
Pray for us!

Pedicab ambulances transport bodies
from the massacre on the Avenue of Eternal Peace.
Nothing stops a tank
except the Tank Man.
In the center of the storm,
inside the ring road, a ring of students ring out,
huddled, hunkered, human.

Each bullet billed to the family of those killed
stings with the serpent's venom
into the wounds of the country's soul.
Timing is everything in this timeless place.
As tanks plowed over hope
and freedom was trammeled, then decimated,
the secret coup set to undo the horror.

The motion was set long before
and the harvest was not about counting grains of rice
but becoming human, aspiring, dreaming dreams

that might come true;
toys that transform:
Old Peking, once shrouded under cypress shade
defiant, dynastic, standing strong with trade —
Gone.

Hutongs boulevarded into oblivion,
towers growing faster than trees,
achromatic clouds, a blanketed brume
a cast and pall of doom:
New Beijing
Gong.

Bronzed street barbers enshrined
like their rickshaw brothers — click!
Smart phone selfies of a time they never knew.

Old men playing games in defeat,
shop signs pronouncing no haggling,
street vendors selling from stainless steel stalls,
caustic cars coursing through incautiously...
and on and on...
Billions want to be the Tank Man.
Every person is a hongbao.

Dove Thy Neighbor

There was queuing on the quays
as droves of doves flew from the jetties
and filed in formation.

As if Noah were watching,
each beak beckoned peace,
bringing crop milk to the newborn
who peered on the pier
at the innocence of broken branches
extended for another go.

Salvation is our salve
on the wounds of sin.
Myths are myrrh,
the sweet cicely of the soul —
through the bird's eye view,
the longing lens of love,
the camphor of the cosmos:
aromatic, aerobatic, erogenous.

The Dwarf

She knows why
and she's told us
but there is a dwarf
who sits and wheels —
steals all attention
from the towering shadow

Remember me
because I will always
remember you
You told us all
in so many words
but you knew
the dwarf knew more

Your eyes searched
but in scant time could only find
a memory of the dwarf
whose unshackled mind
rose from the chair
and stood in the shadow
detached and unaware

Eat or Be Eaten

Bach, van Gogh, Swift

I.

Drifting upon an endless tide,

    transporting me through turbulence,

shifting currents: I am free – my body

    acts as my preserver:

unattached, unfettered, unvanquished

Not unusual, therefore, that I should be

pestered by a natural urge to submerge

beneath the surface: pressured by an

intellectual madness:

seditious, insurgent, eccentric

An opposing force, methodical,

in place in size and rank.

Faces stare up at me from under the water;

faces— billions of faces — with piercing expressions,

which frighten the oxygen from the water;

crowded, surrounded superficially;

shallow, confirmed looks:

The face of regret, the face of fear, of warning;

faces which I know too well.

I'm driven to dive into this sea of unsociable stares,

to scatter the mass, to consume the consuming,

to sink into the community to make a shambles:

Destroy and Recreate!

II.

What is going on?

I ordered chaos!
Chaos dares to order me!

Order is chaos!

Chaos is order!

My mind! My mind!

I'm losing my mind!

FALLING

fALLing

falling

maddening, raving

helter-skelter!

harum-scarum!

willy-nilly!

Looking for a loony,   bin

Looking for a booby,   hatch

Looking for a nut,   house

(so unwanted like this)

Tighten my screw it's loose!

My mind! My mind!

I'm out of my mind!

I'm out of my

out of my

out of my mind!

III.

Oh, look: blue sky!

Harmonious clouds!

Calm waters.

Once in awhile,

we see some ignorant body,

floating, waiting,

for some conversion

(   )

WHAT WAS THAT?

Nothing. Nothing at all.

(hey, I need some help)

Elsa, the Widower

Killed in action,

father and brothers —

Our greatest victory!

The table's too big now,

turned to firewood,

embers aglow with plumes of sorrow

wafting through like fragrance

upon a smoldering battlefield.

Courage delivers tears,

the broth of a thousand memories

stirred into a cauldron whose steam rises

in triumph.

In the snow he trudges

to another day and a different land.

His footprints lead away

but his promise fills her heart

as the snow gracefully

covers his tracks.

It is all fruitless

since the vines

are trellised boundlessly:

Borders changing
as souls ascend.
She can only hope for love
through a war that has an end.

Erlkönig's Tochter

The carriage rambles to and fro,

with father and son warm from snow.

Shadows slink through the dark and drear,

embraced in love, no gloom or fear.

A stunted woman, curved and fine,

luring the boy with love divine;

a siren with a mother's smile,

she waves him to her rank and file.

"A call from the queen," he declares.

But father sees nothing, then glares:

"'Tis just a lantern's fancy foil;

roost and shun that pseudo royal."

"Come, beautiful boy, to my side;

I'll take you home, exit this ride."

"She whispers sweetly, can you hear?"

"'Tis but wind whistling through your ear."

Lovely children dance through the woods,

faces shrouded in devilish hoods:

En'tranced by a macabre mirage —
yet undaunted by each visage.

"See them prancing with capes and cloaks?"
"I see just dark, delusive oaks."
Where goes this dreadful phantasm?
Swallowed deep into a chasm.

"They've gone, dissolved, and disappeared!"
"Is the queen tempting — or now feared?"
Comes the answer — a sudden flood;
his hand rises, covered with blood!

The carriage reels with wild horses
as Hell brings its evil forces.
A father's curse — dismiss his son —
and then behold that life undone!

The Fall of the Stranger

Imprisoned within a vitreous time cell
I cannot find any door labeled [EXIT]
The shifting sandy floor slowly slips away
beneath me, as I fall deeper into time.
The sifting sound echoes through the cylinder
and mocks my frantic flight from the buried truth.
As I land upon an uncharted island
shrill staccato sounds of insect intercourse
reverberates with a Kafkaesque humor.
Facing sheer stark boulders and granular crust
I push a monolith up the mountainside.
My slow uncertain progress fills me with doubt
as the rock religiously rolls over me.
Though I cannot make a conscious commitment
I push the boulder off of my bruised body.
In the stream's cool water I wash off my wounds
and flow up to the peak as the glass is turned.
Tumbling through eons of geologic crust
my fossilized bones clatter and click with fear.
My cramped fingers dig upward through the debris.
I scratch the surface, erode antiquity.
I crawl out of the dark ground and sit on it.
I look around: imprisoned in the time cell.

John Schulte

Flyku

Fluttering about

lovely artful butterflies

paint the colored sky

Swirls and striations

chroma spectral vibrations

iconic memory

Kandinsky rainbows

an iridescent moiré

takes your breath away

Fronts

Beneath the ominous firmament

parades assemble and march

boldly throughout the world

in celebration of global peace.

Peals of thunder rumble

as dankness fills the air.

Thumping drums unite

to beat in time with tranquility.

Lascivious precipitation remains enough

to always disrupt our pompous jubilations.

Tears of relief flood old confrontations

as adversity is washed away.

The welkin opens and swells

to reveal a magnificent azure.

In vain search of desiccation,

there are fights for towels.

Fur Free

Cats
are the most
I n d e p e n d e n t
of all animals…

In fact,
I
own
one myself.

Gingerbread House

HOME SWEET HOME

OME SWEET HOME

ME SWEET HOME

E SWEET HOME

SWEET HOME

WEET HOME

EET HOME

ET HOME

T HOME

HOME

ome

me

e

.

Going Down

We are falling

falling

falling

And we anticipate

pain

pain

pain

For we know what hurts

hurts

hurts

is the sudden

stop

sto

st

…

Hammer into Anvil

Agony
Oh the pain the pain
the pain of it all
Mere existence pounds
itself again and again
face and peen both
claw and head
battering your life
pummeling your persona
striking at your very soul
until you're ready to collapse:
Hammer into Anvil

Injustice
Jurisdiction without power
deception without command
a struggle for truth
a sip of vermouth
Tendered and rendered
the truth: the gavel strikes
the truth: Hammer into Anvil

Knowledge
Rote and recall
Sequence and pretense
Swelling and telling
Drilling is thrilling —
The base and feet provide support.
The waist is a throat
that stops the chokehold
being forged from the fiery
strikes that temper the face
Kachung Kachung
Smashing and bashing
Knowing is done

Reward
Forging is an art
disciplined and seasoned with pain.
Agony becomes ecstasy
once you're insane.
Verdicts, no matter how right or unjust,
can never be all that you trust.
Hot and cold make the manifold
connecting stem to cord
Hammer into Anvil:
Go into your chambers
to find your just reward!

He Knows Things

The unkempt man at the café keeps talking
as he cleans his nails and rakes his fingers
through his wild auburn mane.
And this is what he says —
he says:
"I can't help you because you're
probably an idiot."
He's speaking to a loony looking lad
lost and confused, backpacked with a past
far too profound for someone so young.
The kid hangs in and doesn't get the hint
so the man goes on and on:
"I can tell you these things, kid,
in no particular order. Things that
will change your life.
Get out your pen. Be my friend."
Green Brazilian seeds flutter like beans
through a rainstick and into the grinder.
He savors the moment and inhales
only then to proclaim:
"Humiliation is watching idiots succeed
at what we fail to do."
Espresso took two routes into the shot glass.

The milk swirled into a hot froth
when the man decided to follow up:
"If all is not lost, where is my sock?"
The word sock was pungent and palpable.
The man stood stale and looked around:
"Where is my sock?"
The barista completed her chemistry
and approached the man.
The kid strapped on his backpack
to apply all the wisdom imparted upon him.
He withdrew from the café, scratching.
The man quieted himself, suddenly aware.
He puzzled the barista:
"If there is only one Earth, where are the others?"
She embraced him, offering her tender hands
the way she had offered them a thousand times before.
His rakish manner scared no one as he whispered:
"I try to avoid doing what is going to be done for me."
She handed him a latte as he sat back down,
deeply breathing the intoxicating aroma.
Through the glass outside
the kid could see electrified nerve cells
knitting above the man's head
like the old woman
who feverishly darned his missing sock
in the corner chair.

He Was a Lenin Grad

In the Shostakovich of my mind
drab grey factory stacks
spew green mercury
into young lung sacs
while the red flag unfurls the star
reigning atop the hammer and sickle
revolting against the tsar

Grotesque Mahlerian marches
chromatically kicking against the Great Purge
surge into harmonies cacophonous
coarse contrapuntal chords
billow and bellow brazenly to stifle the venom
mocking hymns of victory play counterpoint
to a myriad of celluloid chintz and banality
bombastically blasting forth to over-score action

In the Shostakovich of my mind
a frustrating frenzy of fiery fretting
and soaring strenuous strains of duress
are caressed by tremulous timpani
as tumultuous storms parade

into the Kremlin — the Soviet cerebellum
the Shostakovich of my mind
where there is no rest in disingenuous triumph

The triumvirate of Stalin, Churchill, and Roosevelt
could not cease the siege upon spirits
until finally a concert swelled out encircling the city,
bloated like starving bellies kept alive by boiled belts
once around their waists, now waifish and weathered
a ragtag band of performers, a skeleton orchestra
playing a calamitous composition of culture and courage
brash Brucknerian brassy and boisterous
a tumultuous testimony of terror
an inquisition for blood
an invasion of slow and ruthless torture
blaring from the bassoons
crying from the clarinets
singing from the strings
dying from the drums
a psychological Squall as shells shot
skyward then downward bombarding back the enemy
premature Nazis champagne-toasted at the Astoria
900 days ended with half a million burials
as six notes descended to resurrect a city's soul

I Vow to Thee

Have thoughts I call my own;
I look up to see God's glory;
I reach up to touch Him.

I dream and see all Heaven;
And I think of angels too;
a child's mind cannot create
that which is not true!

For ev'ry thought a star shines above;
I will find one for peace.
Even if I grow old trying
the hope will always be.

I am young but I am growing;
have thoughts I call my own;
I look up to see God's glory
and then I know —

I know that we're all souls adrift
and God put us here
just to think of all this majesty
that quiets all our fear...

In Between

The crest swells to crash upon the shore.

The whitecap's soft underbelly recedes forgivingly.

In the cleft, as the wave shears apart,

the foam of creation scintillates while

shimmering bliss ripples and dissolves to zero.

Wrestling within every ebb is another flow.

And you emerge, inward and outward, each time,

presenting a perfect heaven.

In the Ives of the Beholder

We speak seven trumpet statements to God,

then do not listen for

answers

in the

silence

between

the notes.

We are the woodwinds

who ruin our harmony by sheer inquisition.

Strings lace time with magic, resolute in mere presence.

Our hearts are percussion, thumping, alive, but hollow.

It is true that truisms deceive virtue.

For behold that when life is going so well,

it can only get worse.

Time is conquered when it runs out.

Truth is a choir of settled souls that sing solo.

And beauty is the suffering of angels.

The Inner Core

In a search, on a quest

we travel east and wind up west.

Trekking around the circle complete,

thinking that the two won't meet,

we start up where we end,

and never quite transcend.

Learn enough to be profound —

then stop right there — don't go around.

Le voyage de l'art

Capricious and confounding —
a cannon so astounding!
Microscope, the king and his son,
shot to the moon from a giant gun —
shelled as a stellar surface stain....
A boldfaced bullet to the brain...
a capsule to the cranium —
no love leaks like uranium.
Selenites' spears greet fearless fools
who pummel down skeletal ghouls.
Bumbershoots pound them to lunar dust
among flourishing mushrooms on the crust.

Brazen terriens give Cosmos pause,
then he condemns with arrogant cause.
Fantasia, apple of the prince's eye,
one bite and she gives love a try.
Snowflakes cascade, a weightless ballet,
while prisoners dance with love delayed,
unconsummated couples erupt,
banished as if morally corrupt.
Magma spews forth a deadly flow

as clair de terre casts its glow.
Then the queen saves their love attuned
on the surface with clair de lune.
Scientists prove that toil makes trouble
while love conquers from the rubble.
Now formed and forged into art's charade
these heroes and lovers on parade!
Behold these wand'ring masqueraders:
Seekers by nature are true invaders!

The Lecturer

Hey, Joe, is it soup yet?
Your image is projected
as we screen your self
standing before us too:
Your persona protected
your anima in an umbra

You are the center
of all consciousness
In this dark room
your character develops
with Polaroid swiftness

I am a variation of Jesus
(That's my soul inside
the circle you drew)
We don't go back
because there are snakes on the moon
Doctor, have you heard?
Only the shadow knows.

John Schulte

Libyan Landscape

Palms sucking like straws

dromedaries filling up

shrinking oasis

Living in Harmony

The tune rings through my ears,

erasing all my fears.

Of all the musical terms, the jargon upon appearance,

still existing in the sound, an expressive resonance.

Even with the bits and pieces

                    in musical thesis —

Of all the staves and notes, dots and lines,

a brilliant passage still seems to chime:

We live enharmonically octaves apart,

dissonant in our minds, but identical in heart.

Knitted together by chords which unravel

it's not the destination but the travel.

Even a world of confusing melody

                    produces harmony —

in this universe of fragmental fractions,

a definite coda urges against distraction:

We live divided when meant to blend,

Our spirits spin the circle to its end.

Lost in Loss

At ease in your eyes
I slip into the pools
and drown in your sorrow
of a thousand cries.
The world is made of fools.
Hope rises tomorrow.

Trembling from the unknown
your embrace knows comfort.
I feel the warmth of prayer;
fear shivers through your bones
holding Divine escort —
a feeling that we share.

Stare to infinity;
look beyond the pain:
Miracles everywhere.
You are the Trinity —
three in one the same.
The devil weeps to care.

Lunar Communion

Sacred Heart blood on the Moon

Body of Christós in celestial bloom

Inspired by the Genesis story in orbit

Buzz turned to the Holy sacrament —

the first fluid poured on the Moon,

a third Body among two men:

Peace on Earth during the deed,

good will and God speed.

M Street SW

The mother ship visits you,
when your meds are wearing off,
gloriously hovering
just beyond the balcony.
But you come to your senses
night after night.
Your dreams orbit around
our logical discourse.
And I believe you see the lights
crystallize into a floating palace,
ascending steps that take you
far from your mother,
further from your sisters,
away from any of the others
who would put you in *there* again.

The last time you vanished
three months passed.
And you emerged with more
meds and less sensations
and lesser visitations.
You stood rocking left and right

like a forgotten buoy
in an abandoned harbor.

Struggling to remain engaged and afloat
you had convinced yourself
there was an underlying balance.
But your body knew the center
could not hold still.
And the craft flew circles
around the tower,
coming to rest outside your window
when you least expected it.

We talked for hours about your
imminent trip: a visit West
to test your independence.
So much to accomplish....
Then there was nothing
for months. And the letters had stopped....
Disconnected in all manner now
until your mother answered my call:
Foul play suspected but only by family,
a closed case otherwise surmised.
Your groceries half-bagged,
the sheers blowing in the breeze,

the sliding door opened,

and an invitation to climb

aboard a life

interrupted or intercepted,

formerly ignored by those who knew you.

I do not see you falling.

I do not see you jumping off.

Like when the snipers were after you

And you ran serpentine, home,

between the buildings on your way from work

Your avoirdupois through a scope

made you an easy target.

You knew they had you in their sights.

And you were always supercharged with hope

through all the regions of depression,

the rippling of your obsessions

you did not know how many

Matryoshka dolls nested your fears.

But the mother ship is not a dream.

They took you and set you free.

And you will never be put *there* again.

The Masks of Revolution
When Truce & Turmoil Coexist

Cameras see more than human eyes;

Eyes pierce through holes of masks;

Masks to camouflage identities;

Identities shielded from gas;

Gas erupting into flames;

Flames of revolution;

Revolution on both sides of the barricade;

Barricades to separate people;

People bonded together by masks;

Masks on the police and protesters alike;

Alike in so many ways;

Ways that are human.

Mmmy Collection of Enthusiasms

That pataphysical Pal gets the capital treatment.

And He says I need an afflatus spark.

I decide to listen up, out of fear and belief.

He's been my Buddy since I can remember.

And now I can't remember when I ever

stopped listening to Him.

So it should never be a matter of dispute

that I'm all over whatever He says.

He says too much is stochastic these days.

And that the New World Order has spun

an imbroglio and web of conceit,

a spider spinning out of control

and catching nothing for all the work.

Literature is dead, He says:

God is Oprah;

His Only Begotten Son is Jon Stewart.

And Camus is right about everything.

Nothing, he says, could be more important

than watching Bill O'Reilly.

He says: The miasma you sense comes from

the rotted corpses decaying

in the graveyard of creation.

That's all your work piling up like bones,

picked and cleaned between the teeth of Abaddon.

Your words rise like wicked ghosts,

haunting the mesmerized minds of no one.

He knows I was on fire many times

and all those inventions are smoldering in the pit.

So why add to that heap, I wonder.

Ponder not, He says. The process is all that matters.

He tells me I should know it's almost over

because the last epic poet died in a motorcycle accident

far away from Homer.

So don't bother to turn the channel:

Demand to see more

because everything is just a click away.

My Dormant PCDH7

I spent time at my grandmother's spinet,

practicing for hours and one extra minute.

My fingers scaled the keys,

did their do re mis,

with fluid ticks and flowing tocks,

a metronome clicked like a clamorous clock.

Time and measures stretch through space,

creeping codas on my aging face.

My maladroit Muse played my threnody.

But rejoice now, my daughter's pure melody!

Lyrical and beautiful, a silken soprano

effortlessly reconnects me to my gram's piano.

For decades, my ability seemingly suppressed,

to be unlocked now, and fully expressed!

This conscious miracle, this created ode —

my daughter is my genetic cheat code.

Norsemen of the Apocalypse

Bones on the moon, pyramids that fly
sure does look like there's doom in the sky
Once you go Mayan, there's no turnin' back
don'tcha think that Quetzalcoatl's a quack?
Swing your hips to the Apocalypse!
Cover your eyes for the solstice eclipse!
Every day is the end of the world
until it's the end of the whirled
any day now…

Dead fish on the beach
beyond Odin's reach
Boundaries that are boundless
through a net that is groundless
I hear the horn from York
surely this signals Ragnarok!

Bones on the moon, pyramids that fly
this could be the day that we die
I never met a Viking to my liking —
belly dancing on skulls
boogie woogie'ing on souls
watusi on the caboose-ee of the train that's gonna end —
but I never met a Mayan who didn't want a friend.

North

I came for the adventure and thrills
and found gold in them thar hills!
Not the nuggets panned and sold
but the gold of grace and majestic old;
of sawtooth peaks cut into clouds
peering out through a Skagway shroud.

Glaciers calve and cleave
as tourists fly in and leave
though fishers copter down
and camp on the frozen ground.
To each his chilling own
as your bones creak and moan.

Fairbanks starts another race
with mushing huskies keeping pace;
calming and cordial, one must salute
the proud and noble Aleut;
garbed in lush vermilion glow
they radiate their warmth atop the snow.

Cannery girls as curvy as the Kenai River
finger out salmon eggs till they shiver;
Ketchikan if you can those Tlingit girls
with their fringed tam hats and white pearls;
and you cannot hope to ever know
the parka perfect women of Juneau!

The men of the Klondike are flannel clad
and have buddies from the west named Vlad.
The ratio of men to women, an 1890s myth —
something incoming singles have to deal with.
'Tis true they embrace the bold frontier —
go where moose trod and have no fear.

'Twas so much fun and so much jolly
ending the Iditarod in Seward's Folly.
I turned to see the vistas once more
from the brisk horizon to the icy shore;
boarding the ship toward home,
I saw the sign: *There's No Place Like Nome.*

A fever fishiness, a quiet insanity,
a place that thrives with exploited humanity.

Overcome

Facing the serpent that dares to strike

staring down a venomous Reich —

to acquiesce in the coils of evil,

to not recoil from that horrid reveal,

affirms a nightmare coalition

that cannot be undone by any contrition.

Seek not to merely repress;

waste not the time to redress,

but take the darkness to devour;

scrub it pure with holy scour.

Curse the cursed and bless the beast;

let evil be served at the godly feast!

Pneuma Moving From Umbra

Some hearts melt and feel complete.

This lone soul can't sense a beat.

Growing old wilts the spirit.

It ends the same to fear it.

A touch of the withered bloom,

a glare from the dying star,

— imminent aura of doom —

awakens the ghost afar.

Public Domain

I am in the public domain
but only as a child;
I am a bloke with a name
who as a man went wild.

As a boy I loved to play with words
and as a man I did just that.
I had my whey and I had my curds;
I was coming back till the rat-a-tat-tat.

Now I am both a boy and a man
not two-faced, as I am who I am.
Innocence lost for a song and a dance
it's a mind game where life is a chance.

Perchance to dream
Yoko just screamed.
It's all the same
I'm still a flame.

A Rilke Romance

My window is an open soul
and I float adrift through the pane
into the star-filled night
to see how far my life will reach.

Space without form, silence without fear
forever reflective like the depth of a crystal
all around me: transparent yet dark
canopied by a veil of unknown proportions.

My heart swells to the cosmos:
The celestial bodies spiral within me
and any one of them is love
so any one of them may float away.

There's one I held; one I began to love:
Of all the possibilities within me
I wonder why this one
an orbit embraced by design, framed by the glass.

There is a fragrance and flight about love:
the stars are redolent ruderals in a meadow
and they parachute and dance this way and that
which makes me stretch into endless reverie and thought:

That the one dandelion I picked is the star I held
with windborne seedlings awaiting a breeze
the delicate sense of love gone stellar
the right one for the right time and space
and all that I am suddenly disperses and disappears
like destiny, into the open window of her life.

Ripples

Empowered by falling bricks,
the warnings breed defiance.
Living history witnessed by a world
in awe of a collapsing giant.

Rising resilience pierces the sky
where humility boundlessly unfolds,
and angels receive their wings
to glide and whisper into deaf ears.

The descending grace eviscerates the place.
Dusk falls till the rise of dawn.
Ashen heaps smolder with plumes of flames.
And when all is gone the steel cross remains.

Knowing where our enemies lurk
the smiles of Heaven should smirk.
Our marauding neighbors turn malicious
and scoff at a nation once propitious.

Face the light from empyrean embrace.
Behold the piety that swells to roseate our hearts.
For the truth of our power is not the height of the tower,
but the strength of our faith within.

Scarborough

The spas were all closed.
It was a soft September
when peace rained upon the
town centre like a fine mist.

Elderly gentle folk
escorting their dogs —
always two on a lead.
There are those who,
when left alone,
find only
loneliness.

Mr. Keith Pedley left
behind a bench on South Cliff
there in a sudden swift jolt there
I stood and understood:
A good bench is a comfort
for many friends you will never know.
And the rescue dogs of Scarborough
are pre-loved bitches who need no collars.

Scandal

A cut to a calf's eye
literal, figurative,
spilling out with vitreous humour
while glaucoma clouds slice the sky.
Eight years later
a man-nun bicycles with his box
and bashes his brains on the sidewalk.
Nothing can put him together
so the clothing recreates him.
But ants swarm through a
crucified wound, and a perplexing
hairy sea urchin nullifies the pain.
Prods and pokes,
sticks and bones,
handily amuse the androgyny.
A striking death and a forgotten breath,
pleasure by the measure,
sexing and vexing,
groping and hoping
ten love cornered
while clanging baby-grands play
the harmony and melody

from rotted donkeys
cradled in the harps.
Faith, tied and befuddled,
eases forward with each pull:
Undertow commandments
from the man-nun can no longer be held,
because of the crushing, the separation,
the anxiety of piety.
Around three in the morning,
martinis arouse all nonsenses.
Punishment is never far behind
when the costume is cast away.
Sixteen years ago
the murder was complete
when the tomes went ballistic.
Falling is a sweet caress across
the naked backwoods where
a corpse cannot find rest.
The genus Sphinx, the hawkmoth skull,
a sneer and a jeer,
while she makes herself pretty
pity the mouthless man
with an axillary goatee,
who gets Medusa's lolling tongue
to slip out as she slips away

to a craggedly coastline
with the man of her dreams.
The shattered box and the remnants
of temptation torn asunder,
a blunder under the current....

In the Spring
when the romance ripples
and each grain of sand
buries the past like a hand,
and the present is not far
behind it becomes all too clear
that time is a thief
like the abrupt end of Tristan,
there is no future in a world
of love and grief.

Schizothemia

With each inch I edge
closer to the crown.
I strain my strength
and bear down
to clamber the length
and traverse up coarse rope
in a most serpentine slope.
Foot atop foot — the only ledge.

An abscissed vacuum
awaits my abdication.
Above the abysmal chasm
my hand clutches the unloosened noose.

I've got to get a grip.
The cord binding us
trembles from taut tension.
Now halfway home
I hang by myself
awaiting coronation.

Screening

Part of the repression came from suppression obsession.

A little let out and lot let in...

seeping while peeping, creeping and crawling,

sticking to the script made a mock true confession.

A curtain curtailed by a curtsy in veil,

kneeling on the nail of the coiffed transgression.

Death in the box, sly as a fox,

whispers and vapors, shadows and souls,

mumbles and madness, troubles untold.

Sin to the wind, blowing with fear,

cloudy repent, yet nearly all clear.

Her spirited cloister now clean as an oyster,

except for what's inside, unseen:

One day it will unfurl —

one day, some day, she'll expose the pearl!

Second Opinion

The gurney wheels flapped like the

butterfly valve in your accelerating heart.

But your brain knew better

as the doctor used his belt strap

to sharpen the scalpel intended

to slice and peel away your face.

His obsidian eyes revealed the snake he is;

slithering into your incisions,

an invader for no other reason than his ego

tells him he is God.

The sutures of his patients are reins

he tugs repeatedly — to show off who's boss.

But your blinders are off,

thank God,

and you see him whipping the nurse

with a prod that belongs in the O.R.

The skull-saw whirrs, awaiting your cap,

but you muster strength through etherized eyes,

and you stare the butcher down,

bringing your soul before what's left

of his rotted carotid humanity.

There will be no blood today, sir.

Not from these veins,

not from this coursing corpus.

He will have to find someone who's all under,

hemorrhaging to satiate his thirst.

You may be gassed,

your hemispheres may be on fire,

but you know enough to keep

the demon from poking into your cortex.

They wheel you away

and there will be another day —

but not another one like this,

for shadows cast doubts,

and this surgeon, it turns out, also has a heart.

Sister

She always wore little crosses

that hung like crimson blossoms from her dress.

Arms outstretched, opened like a bloom

but doomed to die a death through torture

to nurture the future by bleeding into the thirsty earth.

Souls sow like seeds and grow fertile from faith;

she knew misery's marvels through birth

vinegar stained the tapestry

but grace feeds her blessings.

And she rose

leaving behind a cascade of scarlet petals.

Sister Anne Catherine

I ate the tender yellow drupe of Ephesus
while leaning against a stone-built house;
the peeled skin revealed the kernels of the past.
I was moved by this lonely place on the hill,
a plateau of peace near the pyramidal-shaped trees,
where a little stream channeled a trickle of hope
that grew into an orchard of figs and followers.

Amid the rocky caverns,
a scattering of villagers, believers
of a most unbelievable momentous moment,
gathered to see the cypress Y-shaped cross
with its sinewy cedar and palm-wood arms
hanging outstretched in a room like a tombed symbol
of a body and soul that came without congress.

Past two rooms divided by a hearth,
like two chambers of a sacred heart,
through cracked columns of calm,
I saw with ephemeral shivers
the ethereal Sister whose visage was
noble and good, gentle and assuring;

and she bled from her pure wrinkled hands,

from wounds that never heal

drops of precious eternal blood

which promise to bring forth pomes with patience.

The seeds spill into the earth

and grow robust among the thorny thatches,

harvested only by those who hear the chanting,

and pluck the infinite stars like ripened fruit:

Immaculatam Deiparam semper Virginem Mariam,

expleto terrestris vitae cursu,

fuisse corpore et anima ad caelestem gloriam assumptam.

Soliloquy

I am the star.

A cascade, a montage,

a panoramic screen.

The monologue is drawn, slow;

the movement is not synchronous, fast.

My speech is sluggish

whilst my actions move with celerity;

I exist in speeds different than reality.

It is a kind of intimate surrealism,

vaguely incomplete, lacking continuity.

The camera focuses on me: I am the lens:

I see out and into the screen,

though I am never between the fields of vision.

I am in a nowhere sequence

amidst a nowhere scene

within a nowhere frame of mind.

I flashback and forward;

I fade and dissolve.

My mind goes blank.

The screen is darkened.

There is no applause.

I am the audience.

Speckulation

The speck of dust flutters to the floor
knowing it is nothing more
than a fleck of dust
in a whirl of meaninglessness.
In that moment of horror,
in its self-conscious condemnation,
the particle of dust recalls its flight,
its descent through the light
spinning toward utter freedom,
the fluttering terrors of a vast chasm
that tremors with nothingness.
Yet, the dust settles with other dust
and finds queer comfort:
a commingling of misery and mirth,
a farrago of desire and delicacy,
a jumble of grief and glee.
Despair bespeckles and faith bespatters —
the dust, it turns out, matters
— one iota.

Steeping

God is in the teapot

that orbits 'tween us and Mars

Some see and some do not

while others feel the scars

Boiling water scalds

Fragrance wafts through space

Searing flesh through faulds

No one sees a face

But God is in that teapot

with screams oh so lyrical

Absolute zero in each spot

would be a God-made miracle.

THIS IS MY STATEMENT, THIS IS MY POEM

YOU'RE NOBODY TILL SOMEBODY KILLS YOU

YOU'RE NOBODY TILL SOMEBODY DARES...

THIS IS MY STATEMENT:

I'M THE CATCHER IN THE RYE

AND **YOU'RE** ALL GONNA DIE

DIE, DIE, DIE, DIE, DIE!

IT WAS A VERY LONG DAY

JUST AN AUTOGRAPH AWAY

IT'S DARK AND THIS LIMO PULLS UP

AND **JOHN** GOT OUT

HE CAME OUT **THE** PATHWAY

HE LOOKED AT ME

DO IT DO IT DO IT DO IT

I GUESS THAT WAS ME INSIDE

COMBAT STANCE

DO IT DO IT DO IT DO IT

HE'S A **PHONY**

AND NOW HE KNOWS HE'S BEEN SHOT

THOUGH LEIBOVITZ SHOT HIM FIRST

WHEN I CLICK I MAKE HIS STORY COMPLETE

I THOUGHT BY KILLING HIM

I WOULD ACQUIRE HIS FAME

HOLDEN CAULFIELD IS MY NAME

THOUGH I FEEL LIKE DOROTHY GALE

(surrender)

NOW THAT I'M IN JAIL

I THOUGHT BY KILLING HIM

I WOULD ACQUIRE HIS **FAME**

I'M GOING NUTS

AND HOLDEN CAULFIELD IS MY NAME

{IS THAT ALL YOU WANT?}

{IS THAT ALL YOU WANT?}

OKAY, I'M THE **DEVIL** TOO!

I'M JUST A PAWN

CUZ JOHN BEING GONE

IS WHAT WE'RE LIVING WITH

A MYTH IS A MYTH IS **A MYTH**

TURNS OUT IT'S NOT ABOUT ME

SOME DOUBLE FANTASY

IT'S STILL ABOUT HIM, ALL **ABOUT HIM**

WHEN **NOBODY KILLS** SOMEBODY

Today She Rose

You were our treasure
and gave us all you were worth.
You were a gift to us
and wanted nothing in return.

Words have power
In the beginning was the Word.
And words, as you declare,
get into things:
Words got into you and came out
like a singing river rippling
through craggily rocks,
finding a way to stream the truth,
to seek the steady flow
through the serpentine course.

You were an intrinsic mystery
with the pulse of a towering tree.
Vascular roots probing into the settled dust,
delivering nourishment for the tired souls
who boldly used words carelessly.
You, like words, got into things —
deep things, things that were wrong.
But you always found the right things
to end on.

Totentanz

An apparition took my hand,
pulled me to a most cursèd land.
The murky lunar madness shone,
revealing death and barren bone.
The only life was found in Doom,
alive beneath each crypt and tomb.
They moaned the groans of countless souls
entangled in the roots of ghouls.
They tugged at my escort specter,
blood and tears sucked up like nectar.
Down below where shadows don't cast,
amid the dark of demons' past,
deeper still to Satan's death throne,
he slathers on prayers to atone,
devours whole the undead souls
as vipers hiss on fiery coals.
Torment rises with further pains;
infinite corpses dragging chains;
altars with clanging, feasting drones;
trombones gliding with deafening tones;
searing sin scorches hearts impure,
the ghost ends my nightmarish tour.

Triggers

In every thing I have left of yours
I hear your voice; I feel your warmth.
The pocket watch timely ticks
as I hear you talk.

In every thing I have left of yours
I hear your warmth; I feel your voice.
The tools on the workbench collect dust
but they have built an empire.

The keychain tchotchke has such gravity,
and seeing it here brings you back —
unlocking all that was and should have been.

Gone yet not far off but further in,
streaming through my blood,
coursing in my discourse,
and reveling in my mysteries,
I am every thing of yours.

Tubing

The last time I died
the moon was half itself
and I was part mad
while the ocean beat itself
upon the sand

The streets were cold and vacant
like my cells
The clouds were rumbling
and trembling with my bones

The sun did not shine
and I rose like a loon
to the blue neon cross
but Christ was already there

So I left with my mind
while the moon washed the rest
upon the shore

Two Sides to a Story

"Stranger,	"I am
welcome.	no
Where	stranger,
are you	sir,
from?"	than you."

Unfinished Universe

be-re-SHIYT ba-RA eh-lo-HIYM
a water birth floods infinity
softly breaking toward a cosmic pulse
a universe of tone still
percussive and progressive
ripples the celestial spirit
and sets up the impossible:
A medley of maestros amidst
a carom of katzenjammer commotion
fourteen times at the same time
summits of sound saturating the void
like musicians perched atop mountains
melodically mischievous machinations
An unending epiphany
of dramatic narratives....
Mine Ives have seen the Glory!
Gratia Domini nostri Jesu Christi
cum omnibus vobis. Amen.
Amen.
I say Amen!

Unlocking Yourself

Your treasure is always open;
your richness is in your heart.
You are never plundered by touch,
nor robbed of trust.
Your jewels gleam for the jejune
just as they blind the profound.
The influence of your affluence,
the boundless beauty of your bounty,
your abundant spontaneity,
and the gaiety of your spirit —
these are the sacred gifts you offer
to those who have given you
the invaluable fortune of worth.
You are an esteemed being
shining forth faith from the
risky shadow of dreams.

A Very Sublime Night

Chopin's heart does not miss a beat,

throbbing soulfully, but socially discrete.

Immersed in cognac from the darkened cellar,

enshrined within the Holy Cross pillar.

Its rhythm is the cardiac soul

thrumming to cradle and console,

each note effuses freedom and fire,

Polish spirit, fortitude, and choir.

Nocturnes of infinite grace,

joy and sorrow in random replace,

pallid and piquant preludes,

impressive impromptus and etudes,

mucus mazurkas and whooping waltzes,

pitiless polonaises and sibilate scherzos,

sonorous sonatas and coughing concertos,

ballades borne from bountiful bards,

prancing and dancing with covered jards,

rubato ruling and robbing time

all pressed outward from misery sublime,

mingled with resounding romance,

coupled with restless reveries, entranced.

Tortured inspiration between convulsive chords:

A tall figure, transfigured a bent sword

that feels all pain but remains germinal,

thin, gaunt, fragile framed, terminal.

Preserved like a holy relic, this jarred mass

sealed like a seraph under glass;

Euterpe weeps, tears spilling and splashing

onto the strings of a broken lyre, lashing,

glistening gleefully, glowering gallantly,

striking strings of a warm raptured rhapsody.

Penned from passion, his chambers that pass and flow,

his music caresses his Muse, a true love adagio.

Now romanticism rises with people consumed

to play as he did with his heart exhumed!

A Tribute

I pay special tribute to Larry D. Griffin, Ph.D, Professor of Languages and Literature at American University of Ras Al Khaimah, who taught me the terribly wondrous habits of reading and writing poetry. Because poetry makes public the most private of thoughts, because it takes what's inside and places it brazenly on the outside, I asked Dr. Griffin, who instructed me some 40 years ago at the University of Oklahoma, if I could include one of his original compositions which he claimed came flowing out of him while lending his insight and content-critique to this manuscript. One might suspect his sonnet as a mocking tribute, but he is not that sort of gentleman. Or is he? Nonetheless, he consented, as long as I dropped the doctor appellation. So, Larry it is.

That Larry is a colleague, professor, and friend all rolled into one, makes his enamored moment of crafting a poem all the more special to me. We were both at the University of Oklahoma during a time of Visiting Professors like Maya Angelou, Madison Morrison, and Shiv K. Kumar. I learned a profound amount from all of them, but Larry provided me something quite unique — the courage to not just write poetry, but to share it. And to reciprocate that gift, I now, with his kind permission, share his entry from the night he dared to review and provide commentary to this manuscript. Whether he was truly enamored or just felt compelled to write a poem because he couldn't take reading my verbal machines any longer, we will never know. But this much I do know: his poem is a gem, and he is a most gracious mentor.

Red Queen

My then Complete Works of Shakespeare textbook,

now that I look still shows ruddy rouge

on cover, my finger prints of I the stooge,

what I took every day from makeup class

(Daddy thinks I work to make-up a fail;

Daddy his Shakespeare at Northeastern took;

I only apply makeup there to pass),

so I drop Dad a postcard in the mail:

Seat's makeup is right before Tragedies,

so Kabuki white and fingers that look

to fill with other colors without fail

make all colors smear though none relieves

me from telling you my dear when we hear

"The Queen is Dead," smeared in red, no fear.

Larry Griffin, Ph.D
406 Burj Julphar
2 May 2015; 10.37 p.m.
Ras Al Khaimah
United Arab Emirates

John Schulte

About The Poet

John Schulte is a writer and developer of animation, toys, books, and entertainment properties. He served on the development team for the wildly popular *Teenage Mutant Ninja Turtles*. He studied poetry at the University of Oklahoma during the visiting professorships of Pulitzer Prize winner, Maya Angelou, celebrated East Indian poet, Shiv K. Kumar, Dr. Madison Morrison, and Dr. Larry Griffin. He also mentored with Czech scriptwriter, Arnost Lustig. Schulte co-wrote and co-produced a pilot for Garry Marshall, called *Four Stars*. He is the Pop Culture writer for the Los Angeles beat on examiner.com. He co-produced a YA novel trilogy with his brother, called *Time Capsule Murders*. Schulte also edited a host of books by Edgar Award-winning authoress, Barbara Brooks Wallace and a martial arts book, *The 7 C's of Success*, written by Actors Studio alumnus, Shaunt Benjamin. He has contributed to Carolyn Handler Miller's seminal work, *Digital Storytelling*, and Miriam Van Scott's cultural chronicle, *Encyclopedia of Hell*. Schulte is a member of the Authors Guild and the Academy of American Poets. His poetic work has appeared in sundry anthologies, literary journals, and magazines.

John Schulte